The Famous
God Said
Sonnets

D1304854

The Famous *God Said* Sonnets

by

Richard Waller

Broadwood Press
1999

Designed and Typeset by Riccardo Muratore
Broadwood Press

Library of Congress Catalog Card Number 98-93688
ISBN 0-9644320-1-3

First Edition

Also by Richard Waller
Beethoven's Brain and Other Poems   1995

Broadwood Press
P.O. Box 172
Albany, GA 31702-0172

The critical study of the Bible only enhanced my
reverence for the great and good things I found in
the Old Testament and the New. They were not the
less valuable because they were not the work of
"miraculous and infallible inspiration," and because
I found them mixed with some of the worst doctrines
ever taught by men; it was a strange thing to find pearls
surrounded by sand, and roses beset with thorns.

Theodore Parker, 1810-1860,
American theologian and a leading
figure in the Transcendental movement.

After you have got rid of all your dogmas then you
can read the Bible – realize its immensity – not till then.

Walt Whitman

In the first place, God made idiots. This was for
practice. Then he made fundamentalists.

Mark Twain paraphrased.

Contents

In memory of my brother, Gene.

PROLOGUE

Last Sunday morning, sitting in the shade
of my live oak tree, reading Ruth Porritt's poem
meant to be read from the bottom up, my eyes
began on the very last line, as instructed,
and moved against gravity ever upwards and up
and up until I reached the top of the page
and simultaneously the topmost branch
of my noble brooding live oak tree

when a bird of indeterminate species
let fly, with the full force of gravity,
a missile of liquid excreta, an ornithological
bomb of Technicolor poop that splattered
my open book. Thank you, Jesus,
for chastising me. I should have been in church.

THE CREATION

Whoever wrote the book of Genesis
was unaware of the endless births and deaths
of stars and galaxies in a space so vast
a beam of light can't reach the end, God said.
It takes your breath away, but let's press on.
There's nothing about eons of time before
the Garden - trilobites and jawless fish,
Tyrannosaurus Rex and flying snakes,

apes and humanoids and people like
Neanderthals predating Adam and Eve.
It's often asked where Cain got his wife
in a population of three since Abel was dead.
He must have wed the last Neanderthal.
That's why some people don't look good at all.

#3 - Genesis

NOAH'S ARK

Omniscient God, the Bible story tells us,
was taken by surprise one day to learn
that wickedness in men on earth was great.
I'll drown 'em all, God said, but you, Noah,
and your kinfolk. I'll drown the birds and beasts
except one pair of every living thing.
You'll build a boat a little longer than,
but not as wide as, a football field, I said

to Noah, cubitwise. And so it was done
and loaded with billions and billions of weird species
that later Darwin could sort out. It rained
and rained and rained, then stopped. And just in time.
No inside plumbing, or ventilated haven,
sent Noah topside gasping, "Look, a raven!"

THE TOWER OF BABEL

If you believe it, hardly had Noah been dead
three days when a tower arose of mud-brick and slime
that reached high heaven - or was it the lower clouds?
All right! Say three hundred feet. It was built
to immortalize their name lest they were scattered,
but I was not amused at this construction,
God said. I personally dropped in to check it out
and found, to my amazement, the people one,

the language one, and no restraints at all
on doing whatever it was they wanted to do.
Confound 'em all and blast their single speech
into a thousand tongues right now. That's why
all languages are foreign except your own
and those who speak them live in different time zones.

SODOM NIGHTS

One night, two hungry angels came to Sodom
in time to wash their feet and eat with Lot.
It's hard to imagine supernatural beings
famished and tired, or having to wash and sleep.
It's even more surprising that all the men,
not just the fags, but *all* the men in town
showed up demanding that they come out for sex.
No, no! said Lot, assuming the gathering mob

bisexual, I have two virgin daughters
that you can ravish - not my household guests!
It seems politically incorrect today
but guests were sacrosanct, especially *those*.
You know about the fire and pillar of salt.
Affronted angels know when to call a halt.

ABRAHAM AND ISAAC

Tradition has it that I commanded Abraham
to bring Isaac and meet me at the altar
on Mount Moriah to test his willingness,
to sacrifice his favorite son, God said.
Could I have ever earned the reputation
of a kind, heavenly father if I'd behaved
no better than your average prehistoric
despot consumed with human sacrifice?

Instead of being known as founder of the faith,
wouldn't Abraham have been accused
of attempted murder and certified
possessed as one who'd heard the voice of Satan?
If taken literally, would this story matter?
It would. We'd each have been as mad as a hatter.

A DATE WITH DESTINY

For obscure reasons, Moses was not the first
baby bundled in a basket daubed with pitch
and sent down the river to live in a king's household,
God said, I've heard it often told of old.
When he was grown, this famous guest of Pharaoh
stopped a soldier beating up a Hebrew.
When no one was looking, he killed that son of Egypt,
without remorse, and buried him in the sand.

Next day he learned the whole world knew. He fled
those parts for the Midian land to sit by a well
and marry Zipporah, whose father's flocks he kept.
And day by day he neared his date with destiny -
that low-tech meeting in a burning bush.
The moral of his crime remains hush hush.

THE TEN PLAGUES

You, Moses, go at once to Pharaoh
and say to him to let my people go.
Of course, he won't, Your writers will see to that,
God said. They'll say I hardened his heart stone cold
to pass the time and test my bag of tricks.
For starters, the Nile will turn to oozing blood,
the fish will die, and none can drink a drop.
Frogs will slime and swarm in every house,

and lice and flies, and a pox on all their cattle,
and boils and hail and locusts and black of night.
Perchance his heart should soften, petrify it
for the grand finale of death to all first born.
Oh, what fun. Poor Pharaoh, insolent nut
or victim of some writer's disporting rut?

SLAVERY

They want the President to apologize
for slavery, although it's hard to see.
The practice is a clear mistake of Moses
whose book permits a *priest* to buy a slave.
It says that you can buy your bankrupt brother
and make him serve like one of these. Can you
believe the Bible teaches how to treat
your slaves? *Thou shalt hold no man in bondage*

is *not* one of the Ten. And like old Rome,
Allah's traders and Euroamerican slavers
hadn't a holy clue that it was wrong.
It's time to put the blame where the blame belongs:
on a book that says not a word against it, or
what the devil is omniscience for?

CROSSING SINAI

It took the children of Israel forty years
to cross a hundred and fifty miles of desert.
That's clocking three and three-quarter miles per year
or a dusty, sweaty, fifty-four feet per day.
And all they had to eat was manna from heaven,
a small, round, bread-like doughy flake
with a taste like paste no matter how you fixed it -
mill-ground, mortar-beaten, pot-boiled, or fried.

So bland it was they all fell down and cried
aloud imploring heaven to send some quail
to add variety to their repast.
Forty years on thoroughly boring food
no doubt explains why tempers flared to boil.
Such travail, and Allah got the oil.

THE TEN COMMANDMENTS

The priests were perfectly aware that business is business.
I wrote in stone, they claimed, with my very own digit,
God said, rules designed for priestly craft
which any law school sophomore could write.
And like a corporation, chiefs come first -
everyone else is an afterthought. That's why
it took up nearly half, or four in ten,
to say don't mess around with other gods

or worship fatted calves or say god damn
or misbehave on Sunday - keep it holy.
Of six remaining - be nice to ma and pa,
don't kill, adulterate, or steal or lie
or wish you had your neighbor's Mercedes Benz.
Whoever doubts I wrote such things, wins.

MORE COMMANDMENTS FROM EXODUS

In addition to the Ten (they never end),
here are a few on slavery you won't believe,
God said, but try. Now when you buy
a Hebrew slave, six years shall he serve.
In the seventh, he's out of there if single,
but if you gave him the wife who had his children,
he goes out alone unless he swears
how much he loves you, your wife and family.

In that event, tie him down and bore
a hole through his ear with an awl to set him apart
from others less human, and keep him enslaved for life.
Glory be! Isn't Creation a wonderful place?
Of all the Gods long dead or currently active,
who among us is the most attractive?

BURNT OFFERING

Before sundown, God said to the TV preacher,
apply Leviticus 4 to the halls of Congress,
for it has sinned. In order to be forgiven
for the tax code and the IRS,
kill a Carolina bull for me
and pour its gushing blood in a vat where you
can dip your hand seven times and fling
it on the West Front steps and walls.

And cut the fat from the bullock's head, and legs,
and flanks, and muscle meat, its skin and flesh,
and bowel filth, and burn it on the Mall
as an offering to my holy name.
If it's back to the Bible, boys, make it quick.
You want that old time religion? You'd be sick.

MENU, PLEASE

Now listen Moses, God said, here's the deal
on what is fit to eat in my Creation.
It's all about split hooves and chewing the cud,
not one or the other - I won't have it - it's *both*.
Swine, though split at the hoof, don't chew the cud,
so pigs are out and camels, rabbits, and hares.
Fish without fins or scales are bad - no oysters
or catfish for you. And birds! How revolting -

buzzards, kites, and ospreys, cormorants,
storks, vultures, hawks, herons, and gulls.
There's more! No weasels, bats, frogs, or beasts
that walk on paws, but crickets, locusts, and grass-
hoppers are good for you. The list is queer,
odd, yes, but remember who's God around here.

WHY KILL THE GOAT?

If you can, without too much disgust,
God said, read Leviticus 20.
I never said such things. The *priests* said
I said those things, things that irk them most.
Do you believe that I, who made Orion
with its star-birth nebulae and suns
outshining all the rest, am totally destroyed
if you screw a goat? Why kill the goat?

And do you think that I, who said don't kill,
would want to see you stoned or burned to death
for toying with idols, indiscriminate sex,
or seeing a medium before you bet on the game?
You'd do better to study Sigmund Freud
while I attend the worlds beyond the void.

STICKS AND STONES

Of all the things they say I said, God said,
the dumbest is my alleged command to stone
a man outside the gates for gathering sticks
on a quiet Sabbath country day. It's libel
and I categorically deny
ever saying a man should die for sticks
picked up. Whatever do you take me for?
It's unbelievable even as metaphor.

I, who lit the fuse for the Bang
that you call *Big*, have better things to do
in other galaxies than anything
as cruel, savage, and arbitrary as *that*.
It's a wonder the Bible's read at all.
Next Sunday afternoon, go shop the Mall.

FREE SPEECH

Too much of the book of Numbers blasphemes my name,
God said, and the crowning blow is Chapter Sixteen.
It's fantasy, all right, & ahead of its time even
for tabloid fiction. In fact, Numbers was written
by a misle. d dreamer of dreams horrific, a dunce.
I never called down to open the traps of hell
to burn two hundred fifty Jewish leaders
who merely disagreed with Moses and Aaron.

I'm not amused. Nor did I slaughter by plague
fourteen thousand seven hundred souls
who gathered to complain about the death
of those reported burned the day before.
What lesson is this tale supposed to teach,
that I've a low opinion of free speech?

BALAAM'S ASS

The events preceding the beating of Balaam's ass
don't flatter me in the least, God said. You'd think
I couldn't make up my mind or give a command
consistent with a winning grasp of warfare.
Confusion arose when it was reported that I
had changed my mind from no, don't go, to go,
and that I sent an angel to the pass
to scare the daylights out of Balaam's ass.

It fell to its knees and suffered three blows
from the rider's staff while crying what have I done?
Why are you beating me with your staff, Balaam?
Because you threw me! If this were a sword, I'd kill you.
The Biblical writers had a marked affinity
with talking animals and their divinity.

THE MIDIANITES

To all who have read of the killing of the Midianites
without their right minds glazing over, stop!
They bloody well should glaze over, God said,
I commanded no such thing. It's bluster
to claim the wholesale slaughter of *all* the men
and to say that 200,000 women and children
were marched across a desert, with a million sheep,
to Moses, furious that prisoners had been taken.

He ordered, it's written, all boys run through with swords,
and women who have lain with men, but comely virgins
were kept alive for the sexual pleasure of the troops.
And then they blamed these heinous crimes on me!
What kind of ruler of the universe
would I be, if no despot could be worse?

DIG A HOLE

You sing *How Great Thou Art* yet I'm reduced
to saying, allegedly, in Deuteronomy,
that men whose balls are crushed, or cocks cut off,
shall not be allowed to dwell in the house of the Lord,
not to mention shrunk to giving orders
for the proper disposal of bowel dumps in camp.
You shall have a paddle upon your sword
to dig a hole and bury it! *Indeed.*

In making my mythical rounds at night, God said,
and planning for the battle & how to win it,
do you really think my chief concern
is fretting about your crap and stepping in it?
Half-wits eat up Deuteronomy
like grits and greasy balls of hominy.

#21 - Deuteronomy

WRITTEN NOTICE

The fundamentalist church is rigid on divorce,
God said, although the nuts who forged my name
to Deuteronomy make it easy:
just write the wife a note to move along
and marry whomever else would care to have her.
No alimony, child support, and such like
niceties as property division
for one whose fault, no doubt, was lack of technique.

She's free, free to marry another man
but if he does like husband Number One,
she can't go back to him. She's been defiled –
a fact abhorrent to me, I'm quoted as saying.
If Deuteronomy were really mine,
wouldn't it be a little more divine?

THE GRABBER

Don't look in Deuteronomy for gold,
for lilies of pearl or rare red roses of rubies,
they can't survive the air of this gross book
which never could have come from me, God said.
Have you read it? Have you probed its depths?
Have you smelled it? Have you paused to wonder
why preachers never preach, or stoop to teach,
the story of the penis-grabbing wife?

Do you think that I, who made the stars,
would discommode myself about a girl
who grabbed the balls of a villain beating her man
and decree the amputation of her hand?
Is there a lesson here? I think not.
Who dares attribute this to me? What snot?

#23 - Deuteronomy

A FEW MORE CURSES

Not by a long shot am I through with Deu-
teronomy, God said, two sonnets to go.
The poor sadistic fool who wrote with glee
this fiendish book, attributed to me,
should be cooking nicely in some pit
with curses heaped on him who said
I'd heap on you, like curses on his city,
fields, stores and the fruit of his land and loins.

He should but won't be smitten with Egyptian boils,
itch, ulcers, or scurvy, never mind which,
for saying that those who do not heed my words
should be given over to other gods!
You must admit this book is totally stunning.
What kind of heaven or hell think they I'm running?

#24 - Deuteronomy

THE PITS

Towards the end of Deuteronomy,
Moses died. Rejoice that he wrote no more,
God said, my head and heart can barely stand it.
Eat your children? I never did command it.
An insane priest has used my name to scare
the bravest of you with threats of grim-faced nations
swooping down and laying siege until
your highest walls give way and tumble down.

And in my name it's not enough the word
went out to eat the fruit of your womb, the flesh,
the flesh of your own dear sons and daughters,
but the afterbirth between your thighs as well.
It's too, too painful, too utterly painful, I mean,
to put me in a class with Idi Amin.

#25 - Joshua

THE WALLS OF JERICHO

I've always had a problem with my prophets
keeping things fairly straight, God said.
Take Joshua. He fit the battle of Jericho
and the walls came tumbling down, or did they?
The story goes that priests in golden vestments
marched around the city for seven days,
with trumpets blaring, and on the seventh day
the walls fell down. What kind of *battle* is that?

Archaeological investigations will tell you
that the walls tumbled down a thousand years
before your hero, Joshua, was born,
no doubt from a 6 point quake. At any rate,
the blare of trumpets don't tumble walls like that,
not even tuned in G sharp, A, and B flat.

#26 - Joshua

THE VILLAGE OF AI

I want to say, God said, a word or two
about the village of Ai and its defenders
against a Joshuan army of three thousand
inflicting a loss on them of only thirty six.
For a loss of .012 per cent, your hero
tore his clothes and flung himself to the ground
for a dirt shampoo. His revenge would be the death
of everyone in Ai, in all, twelve thousand.

And Joshua hanged the king of Ai on a tree
till sunset and dumped his corpse at the gates.
To celebrate, he sacrificed some sheep
to me, would you believe, as an offering of *peace*.
I do not now, nor did I then, give a penny
for cruelty worthy of New Guinea.

THE DAY THE SUN STOOD STILL

If at some trivia gala they happen to ask you
which miracle was the greatest one of all,
God said, just say the day the sun stood still
for Joshua to kill a few brave Amorites.
This astronomical impossibility
was supposed to have occurred when he opined
that I got in a rock fight with the King
of Jerusalem *before* the place was founded.

I think these early works need some revision.
I never told the prophets the earth rotated
and revolved around the sun at staggering speeds -
too fast to stop without your flying off.
If he thought I did these things, as owned,
I'm afraid poor Joshua was stoned.

THE MERRY SONS OF BELIAL

It's hard to say which book is most barbaric,
God said, but Judges is in the running for the prize.
It makes the story of Sodom and Gomorra
look like a preschool ice cream garden party.
Some merry sons of Belial knocked on a door
asking for the guest that they might screw him.
The master of the house refused, but offered
the pleasure of his concubine instead.

The poor, defenseless woman was abused all night,
gang-raped, and thrown at her master's door at dawn.
He sliced her up with a knife in a dozen pieces
and sent the body parts to the farthest coasts.
This loathsome book, as vile as a lizard's turd,
is called, even now, to my shame, *God's Word.*

THUMBS AND BIG TOES

I'm looking for a possible moral to draw, if any,
God said, from the tale of a battle from which the loser,
Adoni-bezek, fled, and was promptly caught
to have his thumbs cut off and big toes, too.
This mutilated king was nothing if not
philosophical. He said that seventy kings
with thumbs and toes cut off had fought for scraps
around his table, and now it was his turn.

An eye for an eye and a toe for a toe, might be
the moral, a rule of behavior kept to the letter.
It's more than I can say for keeping away
from Eros and a-whoring after other gods.
If any of you in the world today believe
that I inspired this business, no reprieve!

EGLON THE FAT

Some plays of Shakespeare need a stronger plot,
God said. He missed a source they blame on me.
The murder of King Eglon the Fat, of Moab,
by a left-handed man, Ehud, comes to mind.
For showing their asses, the Israelites were condemned
to serve the King of Moab for eighteen years.
Of course, they moaned like babies for delivery.
Ehud came forth with a sword concealed on his right.

I have a message from God, he told Eglon
in the cool of his summer room. He sank the sword
to the hilt in his belly and the dirt poured out & the fat
closed over the blade. He locked the door and left.
In the Pantheon of Gods, does one exist
whose name is stained with such a tale as this?

TRUMPETS AND EMPTY JARS

For sheer insanity, it's hard to beat
the tale of Gideon and his odd fixation
on a fleece of wool, dew-drenched, or dry, as proof
that I would back his battle plans, God said.
His idea was to level an altar of Baal's,
but first he had to vanquish the Midianites
strung out before him too numerous to count
with camels outnumbering the sands by the sea.

To win the battle, he chose merely three hundred,
outfitting each man with a trumpet and an empty jar,
& a lamp within each jar, to blow and smash
upon the signal of a mighty trumpet blast.
Is there any wonder the enemy fled
before an array apparently touched in the head?

THE MILLSTONE

Abimelech is thought to have been the first
mass murderer in history to specialize
in fratricide. His first recorded act
was the slaughter of seventy half-brothers –
some family values! His last recorded act
was the assault on the tower of Thebez
where, you may remember, the Bible says
a woman dropped a millstone on his head.

His skull was crushed, yet he raised up to ask
his armor bearer to finish him off with a thrust
so that no one could say he was killed by a woman.
The soldier promptly obeyed and ran him through.
Another day, another dollar, God said,
Preposterous! The moral? My face is red.

RUTH

After a couple of hundred chapters in seven books
of every kind of vice and folly, God said,
The Book of Ruth, with its four short chapters,
is like a rest stop under the greenwood tree.
Wherever you go and lodge, I'll go and lodge,
Ruth told Naomi, and your God shall be my God.
If she's from Moab, she must have worshipped Baal.
It's gratifying to capture one of his.

While spending the day gleaning in the field,
Naomi told Ruth to bathe, perfume, get dressed,
and wait for Boaz to finish his wine and dinner
and lie on the floor with him in the threshing room.
But sex came after marriage. Ruth was no softie.
At last we have a book that's bloodless and lofty.

ALTAR SMOKE

It's not that I enjoy altar smoke,
God said, it makes me cough. It's more like this:
what better way to furnish priests with meals
than to make the altar a barbecue pit?
The way they did it was this, the offerer
brought up a sheep to roast, and when the meat seethed,
they sent a priestly servant with a pronged fleshhook
to poke around in the pot for his superiors.

The priests made their intentions known, of course,
before the cooking started. Give flesh, they said,
not sodden flesh with fat, but meat that's lean
and give it to us now, or we'll take it by force.
Transactions like these went on for centuries
before they learned the art of saying please.

FIVE GOLDEN MICE

The Philistines who touched the ark to steal it,
lived on instead of dropping dead on the spot.
But after seven months they all broke out
with hemorrhoids and tumors on their private parts.
To appease this God of Israel, they said,
we must return the ark filled with gifts.
Five golden hemorrhoids and five golden mice
should do it, and his wrath shall be no more.

When the ark came home, the people looked inside
and fifty thousand seventy men were slaughtered.
The scriptures say I did it. Would you believe?
Could lies be more preposterous? Perhaps.
If you say I did it, God said, you'll rue it.
I'm here to say I didn't, I did not do it.

BAD DREAMS

For daring to dip the tip of his stick in honey,
Saul said Jonathan must die for he'd
decreed no food be eaten until the foe
was beaten but the people said, not on your life.
To vent his murderous spleen, Saul dreamed
I said go smite the Amalekites, kill all,
man, woman, and child, and King Agag.
Instead, he spared them, all except some trash.

Saul then imagined that I was disappointed.
He cried all night and decided to hack Agag
in little pieces before my sight in Gilgal.
Such was his bloody way of making amends.
If stories like these are taught in Sunday schools,
God said, my book will look the work of fools.

STRAYING FROM THE POINT

No one knows who wrote First Samuel,
God said, except me, and I'll never tell.
He's in disgrace for saying an evil spirit
came from *me* to lay upon King Saul
who gripped a spear while David played the harp.
The object was to pin him to the wall
and kill him, for no good reason, but David fled
and escaped that night to his own house and bed.

Saul's assassins arrived to find an image
in bed with a pillow of goats' hair for a bolster.
He's sick, wife Michal said, and David escaped again.
How exciting, but we are straying from the point.
Is it right to say that evil comes from me?
So much for Biblical inerrancy.

DAVID DANCES

So much of the Bible lies hidden below the surface,
God said, untaught, unread, or barely scanned,
misunderstood and treated by puritans
like thrown rocks that bounce and glance off water.
Now David danced wildly, whirled, and leapt
before me arrayed in his purple linen robe.
He danced in circles spinning around the ark,
and dancing, dropped the cloth for all to see.

Wife Michal raised the window drape and gasped.
She watched her husband dancing by the ark,
dancing naked, and loathed him in her heart:
Now you've done it, now you've shown your hide.
Today, they sing and shout and clap their hands,
but in most churches, no dancing allowed, or bands.

OLD TRANSLATIONS

I'm glad to say some progress has been made,
in clarifying the King James Version, God said,
where it appears that fiendish crimes occurred
when they did not, in truth, thank heaven, happen.
In the case of David's cleanup operation
against Rabbah, the Ammonite city of waters,
he stormed in and brought the people forth
to put them under axes, harrows, and saws,

and passed them through red glowing hot brick kilns,
grisly enough, then went leisurely home.
Now we say he put them *to work* with saws,
and picks and axes, and made them *work* in kilns.
Old translations are often far from right.
They're like a tunnel at the end of light.

FAMILY VALUES

King David lived in a wonderful world of warmth -
fine clothes, hot baths, hot food, warm beds and hearths.
Though wrapped in robes and covered with quilts and downs,
the king was cold, advanced in years, and old.
In a search throughout the land for a pretty maiden,
they found Abishag, the comely Shunammite,
to put in bed with the him to keep him warm.
A fine how do you do, God said, but it worked.

When David died, the widow Bathsheba
implored Solomon to give Abishag
to brother Adonijah for a wife,
but Solomon balked: Adonijah must die.
Not much here in the way of family values:
take other roads, other avenues.

WIVES AND GODS

The sexual prowess of Solomon is amazing,
or should be, if you've given it a thought.
He loved strange women. Call a spade a spade:
Sidonians, Moabites, Ammonites, Edomites, & Hittites.
A *thousand* wives he had, and concubines.
Why isn't the lonely Pope allowed just one?
Yet Solomon found time for affairs of state
and for halving babies for the disputatious.

Another grave concern was the way he turned
to the gods and goddesses of his foreign wives:
Ashtoreth of the Sidonians, and Chemosh,
the abomination of Moab. Passing fancies.
What relevance these stories have today,
God said, frankly I'm at a loss to say.

PISSING AGAINST THE WALL

TV preachers swear, with firm set jaws,
that the Bible is a book inspired by me, God said,
and that if one card falls the whole house falls
which isn't the case at all in a house so vast.
For instance, take the vulgar tale of Zimri,
a drunk, King Elah's captain charioteer,
who, drinking himself besotted, found the king,
and smote him, killed him, and reigned in his stead.

Ordinary stuff enough, but it came to pass
as soon as he sat on his. . . throne, he slew the house
of Baasha, Elah's father, and all his kinsmen:
he left not one that pisseth against the wall.
I don't inspire such words, I'm here to say.
If fundamentalists think I do, they'll *pay.*

FLOATING IRON

For page after page of preposterous passages,
it's hard to top the Second Book of Kings,
God said. I'm afraid the authors got carried away,
away, away, the authors got carried away
in a flaming chariot, like Elijah, ascending
to heaven in a great wind. Seizing the day,
Elisha confiscated his mantle and smote
the Jordan River becoming chief among prophets.

He floated iron on the waters in defiance
of gravity, and *sweetened* the waters with salt,
but stranger still was the child he brought to life
who opened her eyes and sneezed seven times.
In anger, Elisha once made a man a leper,
proving a prophet could burn with a temper like pepper.

CHLOROFORM IN PRINT

Although I am the manifestation of
omnipotence and omniscience, God said,
I must admit I find precious little
to say the about the Chronicles. They're
a dull rehash of Samuel and Kings,
preposterous stories insulting to me, lies,
outrageous fictions, customs inherently stupid
like altar cooking, and bad arithmetic.

And so we'll let the Chronicles go by the boards
as dull, boring, unedifying stuff,
remembering how Mark Twain so well described
the Book of Mormon: *chloroform in print.*
Today, nobody reads the Chronicles,
the Biblical equivalent of barnacles.

SO MUCH FOR EZRA

The Book of Ezra, a manifesto
belonging to the infancy of man,
another age, and time, another land,
is not for now, God said, forget it.
The Christian Coalition licks its chops
over whosoever not obeying this book
could be swiftly judged and suffer death,
banishment, jail, or confiscation of goods.

When the Constitution is abolished,
and TV preachers sing *The Fool on the Hill*,
when Congress and the courts are all demolished,
the Religious Right can work its woolly will.
Theocratic America is nigh,
as nigh as the long-awaited day pigs fly.

ESTHER

Coming as it does after so much
cruel vengeance and bloodthirstiness,
the Book of Esther, like Ruth, is as welcome
as an intermission in a bad play.
Religious content is almost absent, God said,
in fact, I am not so much as mentioned,
& after what my name has been dragged through,
it's a matter of some relief. Enjoy it!

Esther's a novel, like *Gone With the Wind*, but a tale
not nearly so windy. You've only Xerxes and Vashti,
Mordecai, Esther, and Haman to wonder about,
to wonder why they're in the Bible at all.
Martin Luther was so displeased with Esther,
he grew to positively detest her.

#47 - Job

POETS OF SOME RENOWN

Job's Book is the first in which I take great pride,
God said, the first to get it almost right.
This book is great because it's poetry,
one that even atheists can admire.
Although you'll find no answers in the music,
I'm still proud of it. Enjoy your search,
a work among the jewels of the earth.
It shows that I, as a poet, have few rivals.

Shelley and Keats were poets of some renown,
but even they were putty in my hands
when hearing questions posed in the whirlwind,
posed sublimely, but which I did not answer.
If questions pondered throughout history
were answered, where would be the mystery?

DOING A JOB ON JOB

I recall the day some heavenly beings
arrived to present themselves to me, God said,
and oddly enough, Satan tagged along.
I asked, politely, where are you *coming* from?
Proving he, too, could speak poetic, he said,
from going to and fro on the earth, walking
up and down upon it and kissing the ground
that you have trod upon. The flatterer.

The rest of the book is about a famous bet
between us, but Satan forgot the "no touch" rule
and did a job on Job. To no avail.
I won, and sent him back to hell.
Sublime questions follow, sublimely posed.
When will the answers come? No one knows.

POET'S CORNER DAY

At the first annual Poet's Corner Day in Paradise,
the Psalms of David took first place, of course.
A motley bag of loftiness, God said,
and wished-for violence worthy of the mob.
They run the gamut from extravagant hallels,
and grand outbursts of hysterical hallelujahs
to playful similes like mountains that skip
like rams, and little hills like lambs.

Beclouding certain songs and hymns of praise
are cruel desires for vengeance, for ruin,
homelessness, plunder, blood, and death,
for dashing little ones against the stones.
The worth of each is that which it contains,
the good, the bad. Beauty rises and remains.

#50 - Interlude

PSALM 137 IN SONNET FORM

By the rivers of Babylon, we sat down
and wept, thinking of Zion. We hanged
our harps on the willows along the banks,
for they who made us slaves required a song,
and they who broke our lives demanded mirth,
saying, sing us one of the songs of Zion.
How can we laugh and sing in Babylon?
If I forget you, O Jerusalem,

let my right hand wither, and let my tongue
stick to the roof of my mouth if I don't set
Jerusalem above all other joy.
Remember your crimes, Edom and Babylon,
and happy the man who takes your little ones,
throws them, and breaks their heads against the stones.

BETWEEN PRAYERS

The trouble with too many Biblical passages,
is the taint of male chauvinist pigs, God said.
Throughout the Bible, sex is considered unclean;
abstinence, the badge of piety.
Even so, the delights of the female body
are stressed in books like Proverbs where it says
let her breasts satisfy you always
and ravish you with love. Between prayers.

Then come, let us take our fill till morning,
for the lips of a woman drop as a honeycomb.
And as a jewel of gold in a pig's snout,
so is a beautiful woman without discretion.
Reading Proverbs can make the dullest awaken,
but if you think I wrote them, you're mistaken.

#52 - Ecclesiastes

THE HEAVENS LAUGH

As founder, chairman, and chief executive officer
of the universe. you shouldn't be surprised
that I consider Ecclesiastes the Bible's
most appealing and intelligent book, God said.
The heavens laugh whenever backwoods preachers
and unctuous blow-dried TV ministers
pretend to cope with blase rationality,
wry cynicism, and plain common sense.

There's nothing for them to fulminate about,
no covenants, no vindictive prophesies
to make them drool like fools or sing and shout,
just cool advice for quiet, sensible living.
To everything there is a time and season,
a time to play the fool, and a time to reason.

THE SONG OF SOLOMON

I cannot fathom why this is in the Bible,
God said. No matter how you spin it, it's pure
eroticism. I can't imagine it taught
in Sunday schools. It's so against the rules:
HE: How beautiful you are, beloved, how beautiful!
SHE: How handsome you are, beloved, and so pleasant!
HE: Let me see your form and hear your voice.
SHE: My beloved is like a gazelle, a young stag.
HE: How much better is love than wine.
SHE: May my beloved come into his garden.
HE: Open to me, your lips drip with honey.
SHE: I have taken off my dress -
    Stop! God said. Remember, I am pure spirit:
    I didn't inspire this book and don't want to hear it.

THE RAFTERS SHAKE AGAIN

In Isaiah, the rafters shake again
with organ tones of doom. Assyria flexing
its military might had nothing to do
with the wrongs of little Israel, God said.
Like television evangelists today,
Isaiah would claim that I appeared to him
in a dream to threaten dire consequences
if people failed to meet *his* expectations.

An extra-galactic visitor might think
the chosen were evil personified. They weren't.
All people in this garden of good and evil
appear to have an equal amount of both.
The Lord said and *thus sayeth the Lord*
were used so much, Isaiah should have been gored.

#55 - Isaiah

RUMOR DISPELLED

Isaiah used my name to lend an air
of authority to *his* dress code for women,
God said. No mincing about in garments of gauze
foot bells, nose rings, jewels, and bracelets that tinkle.
Instead of perfume, he promised them stench
and warned them of baldness and scabs on their heads,
and said I'd lay bare their private parts
and arrange for their men to fall by the sword,

so many, in fact, that seven women would fight
for each man left, Let us all marry you
and take your name. We'd be no trouble whatever
as long as you save us from being old maids.
You've heard it said the Bible has no humor.
Doesn't this madness dispel that rumor?

#56 - Isaiah

SIX WINGS

A word about dreams that portend the Revelation,
God said, the cosmic nightmare that ends the Book.
The really weird ones began with Isaiah's vision
of my seat in heaven the night Uzziah died.
Hovering over me were six-winged angels:
that's three pairs of wings, one more than dragonflies.
With two of their wings, they covered their faces;
with two others their feet; and with two they flew.

Six wings play havoc with aerodynamics, but it
was only a dream. One angel flew over the altar
with a pair of tongs and picked up a burning coal
to touch Isaiah's lips to forgive his sins.
Not even fundamentalists abuse
our ears with images of such small use.

#57 - Jeremiah

OMNISCIENCE CONTRARIWISE

If people in trouble look in the Book for help,
God said, I trust they won't turn to Jeremiah
in the expectation of comfort and clear understanding
they're taught to expect. It's hard to find the gold.
I am alleged to have had a conversation
with Jeremiah about the rod of an almond tree
and a tipping pot, the meaning of which your guess
is a good as mine, omniscience contrariwise.

Despite the confusion, the message was simple:
the northern tribes would waste the southern tribes
because I caught them sporting with other gods,
but it took them seven long chapters of poetry to say so.
If a God was described as I was supposed to be,
is it any wonder they turned from me?

#58 - Jeremiah

EARTHQUAKES

In Jeremiah, you'll see it plainly states
that when I'm angry, earthquakes happen. Bosh!
Erroneous verses that say I cause disasters
when angry belong to the late Stone Age, God said.
I trust by now that you have passed that stage
and have some knowledge of geology,
of violent waves of energy that flow
in shifting rock formations far below.

In all, a million and a half people have died
in quakes in your century alone.
No god, not even one from Bora Bora
could get *that* mad, and therein lies the rub:
it raises the question of Biblical inerrancy,
but that's all right. It's errant, believe you me.

A TALE OF TWO CITIES

How lonely sits the city that was full
of people. How like a widow she has become,
she that was great among nations. A common lament,
good poetry: Paris, 1940?
It's about the Fall of Jerusalem
to the military might of Babylon
in 587 B.C. The defeat was blamed
on me, God said, as punishment for its sin.

How tiresome, how very, very tiresome!
Almost every disaster has been blamed
on my displeasure instead of the natural world
or the superior forces of another country.
Thank goodness for the age of science and reason.
Religious superstition has had its season.

#60 - Ezekiel

WHEELS WITHIN WHEELS

Ezekiel described four living creatures that looked
like a man with eight sets of wings and a quartet of heads,
each having the face of lion on the right, and an ox
on the left, were somehow connected to a wheel.
The wheel had wheels within wheels, leading New Agers
to believe Ezekiel was zapped by a UFO,
God said, he may have been: surely you know
he saw a valley of dry bones rattle up and dance.

Nevertheless, he almost ran out of threats
he said *I* made, and the above described monster,
whatever it was, was supposed to look like me,
to be the very spit and image of me.
If uglier creatures exist, can you name them?
If people turn away, can you blame them?

#61 - Ezekiel and Psalms

DISCRETION ADVISED

In Psalms where it says he smote the hinder parts
of his enemies, it means he beat their asses,
God said. It often happens that euphemisms
are thrown to the wind for bowels, piss, and dung.
Ezekiel says you'll dine on barley cakes
baked with human dung. In Isaiah
you'll read of eating it, and drinking piss,
and of tables filled with vomit and filthiness.

How the fundamentalists avert
their eyes from this outrageous vulgarity
and claim these words were inspired by me
I don't know, omniscience notwithstanding.
In church, or in refined company,
it's risky to read the Bible randomly.

SHOW TIME

The book of Daniel is full of theatrical drama,
God said, beginning with a burning, fiery furnace
and suspension of a basic law of thermodynamics
which says that fire is no respecter of persons.
There are visions and dreams: Nebuchadnezzar's crackup,
Belshazzar's Feast, and the handwriting on the wall
in a language known to none but Daniel
which freed him for his own interpretation.

And there's the lions' den with Daniel in it -
at 90, no fresh morsel for hungry cats;
and enigmatic nightmares of apocalyptic
beasts of a time, two times and half a time,
whatever, and a foretaste of the Revelation,
the chief insult to me in all Creation.

#63 - Jonah

A HEAD FULL OF SEAWEED

No minor prophets, please, in this series,
except for Jonah whose head was full of seaweed
before his cruise in the whale's belly, God said,
as were the authors of this preposterous tale.
The Mediterranean is not the home of whales,
and there are no whales anywhere
dumb enough to swallow a prophet who'd spend
three days in its belly praying to me in poetry.

Consider this fish tale a whopper, as well as his trip
to Ninevah and its surrounding woods
where he made himself a booth with roof
of gourd withered by a worm sent by me!
Nothing in the canon is this inane.
To say that I inspired it is insane.

EPILOGUE

And so we come to the end of our little tour
of a book about the first four thousand years
of civilization at the end of the Inner Sea,
a world bestseller worshipped like a charm.
Denial ain't just a river in Egypt,
as rappers say, it's a problem many have
when reading the Bible for enlightenment
only to find it's often preposterous.

How could it be? Easily, God said,
it wasn't inspired by me in its entirety.
You must use the intelligence I gave you,
when reading it, to know what's truly mine.
Like panning for gold, you must sift it well
to find great nuggets in heaven or in hell.

Index of Titles